Martin Luther's Ninety-Five Theses

Introduced and Edited
by Stephen J. Nichols

P&R PUBLISHING
P.O. BOX 817 • PHILLIPSBURG • NEW JERSEY 08865-0817

Printed in the United States of America

Illustrations on pages 7 (Martin Luther, 1520) and 13 (Unused Indulgence Slip, 1515), courtesy of the Pitts Theology Library, Candler School of Theology, and used by permission. The illustration on the cover and page 19 (Wittenberg, 1546) has been reproduced from Julius Theodor Köstlin, *Life of Luther* (New York: Scribner's, 1913), p. 537.

Library of Congress Cataloging-in-Publication Data

Luther, Martin, 1483–1546.
    Martin Luther's ninety-five theses / edited by Stephen J. Nichols.
        p.   cm.
    Includes bibliographical references.
    ISBN-10: 0-87552-557-1
    ISBN-13: 978-0-87552-557-0
    1. Luther, Martin, 1483–1546. Disputatio pro declaratione virtutis indulgentiarum. 2. Indulgences. 3. Reformation—Germany—Sources. I. Nichols, Stephen J., 1970– II. Title.

BR332 .D6 2002
230'.41—dc21

                                            2002066226

CONTENTS

LIST OF ILLUSTRATIONS

INTRODUCTION

Tradition has it that one evening Martin Luther, while walking the streets of Wittenberg, happened on a parishioner lying drunk in the gutter. As Luther rebuked him for public drunkenness, his parishioner fumbled around in his coat. Finally his hand emerged holding a piece of paper. He waved it before his priest, proclaiming that Brother Tetzel had issued him an indulgence that offered "complete forgiveness of all sins—past, present and future." Such a scene, as depicted in the 1955 classic, black-and-white film *Martin Luther*, may be difficult to verify. It illustrates, however, the dilemma facing the young parish priest and theologian. In response, Luther retreated to his study, wrote a list of arguments to address this problem, and the next day, October 31, 1517, nailed his list to the church door at Wittenberg.

Little did Luther realize the outcome of his action. By confronting the medieval Roman Catholic Church, he was challenging one of the largest political and ecclesiastical machines the world has ever seen. His action on that last day in October set the stage for a century of upheaval in Germany and across Europe. In fact, repercussions of Luther's actions still ring out today. All who call themselves Protestants trace their roots to this protest in the *Ninety-Five Theses*.

Martin Luther intended that these arguments, written in Latin, be directed toward church scholars for debate. He prefaced his arguments with a request that "those who cannot be present to debate orally with us will do so by letter." That debate never materialized. The arguments, entitled *Disputation on the Power and Efficacy of Indulgences* and known popularly as the *Ninety-Five Theses*, were translated into German, printed (the printing press had been developed relatively recently), and rapidly circulated throughout the cities and villages of Germany. This was only the beginning: by posting the *Ninety-Five Theses*, the young Augustinian monk set in motion one of the most significant events of western history, the Protestant Reformation.

The *Ninety-Five Theses* is a text that everyone knows of, most refer to, but few actually read. Such a crucial text, though, deserves to be read widely. Today's readers might be surprised that the arguments lack the crystallized expression of the later Reformation doctrines, such as justification by faith alone. Also, Luther assumes his readers are aware of medieval theology, as well as events of the first two decades of the sixteenth century. Consequently, this edition offers explanatory notes to help readers navigate the text. To set the *Ninety-Five Theses* in its historical context, we begin with a brief look at the life of Martin Luther and the events in and around 1517.

I Will Become a Monk

One of the best ways to understand Luther is through the German word *Anfechtung*. This daunting

Woodcut of Martin Luther (1520)

word refers to an inner struggle, temptation, or even attack. In Luther's case it applies to his spiritual struggle, the soul anxieties that filled him with intense unrest. Luther's spiritual struggles began before he entered the monastery. On one occasion, returning home from his studies at the University of Erfurt, he encountered a violent thunderstorm. He looked for shelter and in desperation called out to St. Anne, the patron saint of mining (his father's occupation), to save him. "Help me, St. Anne," Luther cried, "and I will become a monk." As historian Roland Bainton remarked, she kept her promise and he kept his. At the monastery, however, he continued to live under the clouds of a spiritual tempest.

Luther dedicated himself wholly to the church and the regimen of monastery life. In his own later reflection, he claimed he was such a good monk that "if ever a monk could get to heaven by monkery, I would have gotten there." But his spiritual unrest continued as he failed to find the forgiveness and salvation he so earnestly desired. He wrote in despair, "I hoped I might find peace of conscience with fasts, prayer, vigils, with which I miserably afflicted my body; but the more I sweated it out like this, the less peace and tranquillity I knew."

He also became increasingly aware of the hypocrisy and inefficacy of the institution he so revered. Anticipating a spiritual haven on a pilgrimage to Rome in 1510, Luther found the city to be more like Vanity Fair in *Pilgrim's Progress*. He reached a crisis point on the steps of Pilate, which had been relocated to Rome. Crawling up and down these steps on his hands and knees, Luther uttered the Lord's Prayer on every step and on every step felt himself drifting further and further from Christ's salvation.

Disillusioned, Luther returned to Wittenberg. His compulsive confessing nearly drove his confessor and mentor, Johann Von Staupitz, mad. Staupitz thought Luther needed a distraction, so he sent Luther to gain his academic degrees and become a theologian and professor. This did not work—Luther's study only intensified his anxiety. On one occasion he went so far as to say that he hated God. He hated God because he lived in utter fear of him and his righteousness. The church offered him no remedy. He tried, probably as hard as anyone in history, but he could not attain the standard that God's righteousness demands. He could find no forgiveness of his sins and no deliverance from God's wrath.

Indulgences and the Sistine Chapel

Luther's contemporaries were not so vexed. They accepted the church's remedy: indulgences. Not new to the church, indulgences were first instituted during the time of the Crusades. The church considered those who went on the Crusades worthy of certain merits and graces, and it dispensed such blessings upon them. But not every person wanted to go, or for that matter could go, on the Crusades. The church made it possible for such people to receive these blessings by sending money instead. So began the buying of indulgences.

The selling of indulgences grew out of the medieval sacrament of penance, which entailed four steps: contrition, confession, satisfaction, and absolution. Contrition involves sorrow for sin, which is then expressed in confession to the priest. Next follows satisfaction (a work of merit) such as fasting, prayers, or giving alms. It is called satisfaction because it satisfies God for the sin committed. The priest then announces absolution or forgiveness, as the power of the gospel is particularly applied to the sin confessed. Eventually the practice of satisfaction grew to include the purchase of indulgences, which soon replaced contrition and confession as well.

But the indulgence Luther encountered in the fall of 1517 was unlike any preceding it. To understand it, we need to return to Rome. Pope Leo X (1513–1521), from the renowned Medici family of Florence, was a patron of the arts. Determined to make Rome in general and St. Peter's Basilica in particular cultural monuments, Leo commissioned many of the attractions that astound modern-day visitors to Rome. He enlisted the services of Raphael and Dürer and of Michelangelo to paint the Sistine Chapel ceiling. Leo X's letter to Raphael in 1515 expresses his goals for St. Peter's Basilica:

> We now have no greater desire than that the entire sanctuary be completed as quickly and as magnificently as possible: we appoint you the architect of this building and grant you a sum of three hundred gulden. . . . Finally I admonish you in the discharge of this task assigned to you, you proceed in such a manner that everyone will see that you have not lost sight of the good reputation for which you had to lay the foundation in your youth, nor of the

hope which we place in you, and of our paternal good will toward you, nor of the dignity and fame of this sanctuary which has always been the holiest and greatest in the world, nor finally, of the reverence we owe the prince of the Apostles.

The building, sculpture, and painting, however, came at a considerable cost, which depleted the church treasuries. Leo X needed money. Fortunately, Albert of Mainz needed another title. He had already acquired two bishoprics and now wanted to be named Archbishop of Mainz. By canon law, Albert could not hold this post while retaining his other titles. He needed a papal dispensation. Eventually the two agreed on a sum that would ensure Albert his position and would also ensure Leo X his funds. The only remaining problem was that Albert's wealth was primarily in land instead of currency. To escape this dilemma, Albert turned to his monk, Johann Tetzel. Tetzel devised a scheme to raise the money by an unprecedented sale of indulgences. Leo X granted his blessing, he added his imprimatur to the indulgence, and Tetzel began selling his product.

Tetzel's indulgence promised complete forgiveness of past and future sins. It promised absolution of sins without contrition or true repentance, and it offered absolution without satisfaction, or works of merit. Instead, one could simply buy satisfaction for sin. This abuse of the sacrament of penance confounded Luther. Consequently, a large number of his ninety-five theses challenge Tetzel's practice against the standard of the church's dogma.

Tetzel's indulgence also promised to free a soul from purgatory. This was quite a selling point. Imagine the chance to save one's father, mother, grandparents, or even child, from the terrors and misery of purgatory. To underscore this benefit to buyers, Tetzel prepared sermons containing vivid descriptions of the horrors of purgatory for parish priests to preach just before he entered their towns. Included in the sermons would be depictions of suffering relatives desperately reaching out for help and deliverance. Then Tetzel would arrive for the sale.

Tetzel even devised a marketing jingle emphasizing this benefit. The English translation reads,

> Every time a coin in the coffer rings,
> A soul from purgatory it springs.

The indulgences, as the jingle reveals, did come at a cost. In fact, it was such a high cost to German peasants that in one of his ninety-five arguments, Luther exclaimed that if the pope knew the toll that the indulgences were taking on the poor, "he would rather that St. Peter's go to ashes, than that it should be built up with the skin, flesh, and bones of his sheep."

Still, the indulgences found a ready market. People traveled to Albert's district to purchase them. Even Luther's parishioners, as the earlier anecdote illustrates, crossed the Elbe River and handed Tetzel his fee. Since the indulgences warned that any priest who would not recognize their power was subject to excommunication, Luther faced a difficult decision. Unable to remain silent, he entered the fray.

Albertus Dei et Apostolice sedis gratia Maguntinen. et Magdeburgen. Archiepiscop9 ac Halberstaten. ecclesiarum Administrator/ Germanie Primas/ sacri Romani Imperii Archicancellari9 princeps elector Marchio Brandenburgen/ Stettinen/ Pomeranie/ Cassuborü/ Sclauorumq Dux. Burggrauius Nurenbergen Salutem in domino.

Sincera feruentisq deuotio quam ad Romanam ecclesiam et fabricam immensi operis Basilice Sancti Petri de vrbe gerere comprobaris/ ex quo iuxta ordinationem per nos factam ad illius reparationem debitam fecisti contributionem merito nos excitat et inducit vt petitionibus tuis illis presertim quas ex deuotionis feruore prodire conspicimus fauorabiliter annuam9. Dinceps q̄ nos tuis deuotis supplicationib9 inclinati. Vt liceat tibi habere altare portatile cum debitis reuerentia z honore sup̄ quo in locis ad hoc congruens z honestis sine iuris alieni preiudicio. Et si ad loca ecclesiastico interdicto ordinaria auctoritate supposita te declinare ztigeri: in illis clausis ianuis: excommunicatis et interdictis exclusis: dummodo tu causam nō deberis interdicto: quoq̄ viseris per te ipsum vel per ppriū aut alium sacerdotem idoneum secularem vel regularem quouis anni tempore preterq̄ in Pasch̄ate missam etiam ante diem circa tamen diurnā lucem celebrari seu celebrari facere possis. Quodq̄ aliquā vel aliquas ecclesias per te eligendas deuote singulis Quadragesimalib9 et aliis diebus quibus ecclesie vrbis et extra eam p̄ christifideles p̄ consequendis Indulgentiis stationū vrbis visitari solent visitando : tot z similes Indulgentias et peccatorū remissiones consequaris quas consequereris si singulis diebus eisdem dictas ecclesias personaliter visitares. Corpusq̄ tuum ecclesiastice sepulture cum funerali pompa tempore Interdicti quauis auctoritate apposito dūmodo tu causam nō deberis Inter dicto tradi possit auctoritate Apostolica qua p̄ spēales Sctissimi dn̄i nostri Leonis diuina p̄ouidentia Pape decimi literas fungimur deuotioni tue de spēciali gratia Indulgem9. Prouiso tamen. Quod p̄cethuiusmodi in bulto ante diem celeb:arob̄ seu celeb:ari facieno vtaris. Quia cum in altaris officio immoletur domin9 noster Jhe sus Christus dei filius : qui cando: esfulgis eterne /congruit ip̄ non noctis tenebris fieri sed in luce. In quorum fidem presentes literas fieri dictaq̄ fabrice Sigilli iussimus appensiō communiri. Dat9   Anno dn̄i

Mcccc.xv   Die

Densis   pontificatus prefati dn̄i nr̄i Pape Anno

The Road to Reformation

A few main concerns dominate Martin Luther's *Ninety-Five Theses*. First, Luther finds that Tetzel's indulgence sale runs counter to the church's dogma concerning the sacrament of penance. Throughout the document, Luther demonstrates how this false practice harms the pope and the laity, and how it injures the Word of God. He calls the indulgence sale blasphemous. He also specifically addresses Tetzel's claim that the indulgence will free dead souls from purgatory. If the pope, Luther argues, had the ability to free souls from purgatory, then why would he charge to do so? If it is truly within his power, then he should waste no time in emptying purgatory without charging a fee. Many of the arguments concern themselves with this and similar points as Luther engages the question of purgatory, the pope's power, and the abuses of indulgences.

These concerns, however, were only window dressing. Luther mentions his fundamental concern in his very first argument: What is true repentance? Put in a way that relates to Luther's lifelong struggle: How does one receive forgiveness of sin? On this basic point Luther and the medieval Catholic Church were worlds apart.

"The true treasure of the church," Luther writes, "is the most holy gospel of the glory and grace of God." The peace of God comes not through indulgences, he argues, but through the cross. He is beginning to see that God's righteousness is not something he earns, but something Christ has achieved for him. His *Anfechtungen*, his soul struggles, are soon coming to an end. By his own admission, his understanding of the essential principle of Reformation doctrine, justification by faith alone, will take until 1519. The *Ninety-Five Theses* begins us on the road to Reformation, but we have not arrived there yet.

As you read through the document, you will notice that while questioning the church, Luther still endorses cardinal Catholic doctrines. He is critical of Tetzel's indulgence sale, but he does not condemn all indulgences. Further, he endorses the doctrine of purgatory. In the preface to an edition of his own works in 1538, Luther attacks the shortcomings of his *Ninety-Five Theses*. He confesses his "folly, ignorance, and infirmity" for honoring the papacy and indulgences: "I did not know many things that I know now." He continues, "For who was I—a wretched little brother then, more like a corpse than a man—to oppose the majesty of the Pontiff?"

Despite its limitations, the *Ninety-Five Theses* demanded the attention of the entire church. Catapulted into controversy, Luther met challenges, criticism, and misrepresentations. To counter them he wrote a thorough discussion of each thesis in *Explanations of the Disputation Concerning the Value of Indulgences* (1518). Unlike the *Ninety-Five Theses*, which was written in a remarkably short time, this document required months of revising before Luther thought it ready to go to print. *Explanations* is a commentary on the *Ninety-Five Theses*.

His explanation and defense of thesis 62, which reads, "The true treasure of the church is the most holy gospel of the glory and grace of God," stands as a good example of how his *Explanations* both clarifies and defends his thought. Here Luther observes that the "gospel of God is something which is not very well known to a large part of the church." It has become obscured, he argues, and eclipsed by discussions of indulgences and merit, or earning one's salvation. He then notes: "According to the Apostle in Romans 1, the gospel is a preaching of the incarnate Son of God, given to us without any merit on our part for salvation and peace. It is a word of salvation, a word of grace, a word of comfort, a word of joy, a voice of the bridegroom and the bride, a good word, a word of peace." He concludes: "Therefore the true glory of God springs from the gospel. At the same time we are taught that the law is fulfilled not by our works but by the grace of God who pities us in Christ and that it shall be fulfilled not through works but through faith, not by anything we offer God, but by all we receive from Christ and partake of him." Though *Explanations* does not enjoy the recognition of the text that it explains, it offers important insight into Luther's formative thought.

The *Ninety-Five Theses* clearly marks the beginning of Luther's quarrel with Rome. As one can imagine, Leo X was unreceptive to the young German monk's criticism. Eventually in 1520 the pope issued a papal bull, *Exsurge, Domine* ("Arise, O Lord"), excommunicating Luther. In typical fashion, Luther publicly burned the document that condemned him as a heretic. He also continued his writing, and in October 1520 he produced a sustained criticism of the church. This work, commonly referred to as *The Three Treatises*, includes *Address to the German Nobility*, *The Babylonian Captivity of the Church*, and *Freedom of the Christian*. In November Luther's pamphlet *Against the Detestable*

Bull of the Antichrist was published in Germany. Luther's quarrel with the church reached a zenith.

Luther was summoned before the Diet of Worms, a regular assembly of both ecclesiastical and political officials at the German city of Worms, April 16–18, 1521. Here he refused to recant his writings, exclaimed that his conscience was held captive to the Word of God, and boldly proclaimed, "Here I stand." It was also here that Luther was condemned to death. Frederick the Wise, ruler of Wittenberg and Luther's admirer, arranged for him to be kidnapped and kept out of sight so the diet's ruling could not come to fruition. Luther hid for almost one year in Frederick's castle at Wartburg before returning to Wittenberg, where he resumed teaching at the University of Wittenberg and preaching at the city church. The significant difference: Luther no longer served as an instrument of the Roman Catholic Church.

In 1525 Luther married Katherina Von Bora, a former nun. Together they had six children and adopted four more. Luther affectionately referred to his wife as "Katie, my rib." They made their home in Luther's former monastery, which Frederick the Wise had given him. The large house afforded the opportunity for many gatherings. Traveling dignitaries and students at the university frequently found themselves around his table discussing theology, singing hymns, and simply learning from Luther's example as he lived out his faith in plain view.

During these years Luther wrote, lectured, preached, and administered the new church. During his year of exile at Wartburg, he had begun translating the Bible into German; by 1534 Germans for the first time could read all of Scripture in their own language. His other works include *The Bondage of the Will* (1525), catechisms and confessions, numerous commentaries on biblical books, and hymns (including "A Mighty Fortress Is Our God").

Luther's legacy also includes the church that bears his name. He devoted much time to supervising the fledgling evangelical church in Germany. In fact, he died in the town of his birth, Eisleben, having gone there to settle a dispute between the church and the town. He became gravely ill and died on February 19, 1546.

Just a few days before he died, Luther wrote his last letter to Katie. Then he wrote his final words on a scrap of paper. He referred to the supremacy of the Bible, noting "we should bend low in reverence before it." He ended his note, dated February 16, 1546: "We are beggars! This is true."

At death, Luther no longer feared or hated God. Instead, in humility and dependence he stood before God accepting his gift of forgiveness and redemption. In the preface to a 1545 edition of his writings, Luther recalled the theological breakthrough that resulted in his conversion: Paul's words in Roman 1:17, "The righteous shall live by faith," were the "very gate to paradise." Where once Luther both raged against.and trembled under the thought of the righteousness of God, now he extolled these, "the sweetest of words."

Martin Luther's legacy continues to enrich the church through his writings, through the various branches of Lutheranism, and through Protestantism. All of this may be traced back to the last day in October 1517 and the nailing of the *Ninety-Five Theses* to the church door.

Wittenberg on the Elbe River (1546). Reproduced from Julius Theodor Köstlin, *Life of Luther* (New York: Scribner's, 1913), where it is said to be "from an old engraving."

NOTE ON THE TEXT

Although Martin Luther wrote the original *Ninety-Five Theses* in Latin, German translations and numerous reprints followed. Further translations, including texts in English, have been coming off the press since the sixteenth century. Today the document is one of the most prominent texts in western church history. The text that follows is loosely based on the English translation of Adolph Spaeth, L. D. Reed, and Henry Eyster Jacobs. At places I offer my own renderings of their text, providing a readable English version while striving to preserve the intent of the original.

Ninety-Five Theses

Disputation on the Power and Efficacy of Indulgences

October 31, 1517

1   The quote from Matthew 4:17 comes from the Vulgate, the authoritative Latin translation. The Latin reads, *Penitentiam agite*, which may be translated, "Do penance." Thus this translation lends credence to the medieval Roman Catholic sacrament of penance. In his *Explanations of the Ninety-Five Theses* (1518), Luther notes that the Greek text means simply "repent," as translated in most English versions of the Bible. Luther is arguing that penance, or merely outward acts, is not in accord with scriptural teaching concerning the forgiveness of sin. True repentance, or that which God requires, is a heart change followed by a life of obedience. The next three theses address the question of repentance. Luther makes his point clear: buying indulgences is in no way equivalent to inward repentance.

2   In 1439 at the Council of Florence, the Roman Catholic Church sanctioned seven sacraments: (1) baptism, (2) confirmation, (3) priesthood or ordination, (4) the eucharist or the Lord's Supper, (5) marriage, (6) extreme unction or last rites, and (7) penance or confession. Luther, along with the other Reformers, reduces this list to the two biblically sanctioned sacraments of (1) the Lord's Supper and (2) baptism. Luther's point in this thesis and those that follow is that the current practice of indulgences is an abuse of the doctrine of penance.

3   Luther sees the connection between the inward change of heart and the external life of obedience, which he characterizes here in the language of Romans 6–7 as putting the flesh to death. Throughout his writings Luther addresses this same issue, but uses the terminology of law and gospel. Typically he is interpreted as emphasizing gospel and deprecating law, especially after salvation. His emphasis on the life of obedience here, however, needs to be considered in the discussion.

Out of love for the truth and the desire to bring it to light, the following propositions will be discussed at Wittenberg, under the oversight of the Reverend Father Martin Luther, Master of Arts and of Sacred Theology, & Lecturer on these subjects at Wittenberg.

Wherefore he requests that those who are unable to be present and debate orally with us, may do so by letter.

In the Name of Our Lord Jesus Christ. Amen.

1. When our Lord and Master Jesus Christ said "Repent," he intended that the entire life of believers should be repentance.

2. This word *repentance* cannot be understood to mean the sacrament of penance, or the act of confession and satisfaction administered by the priests.

3. Yet it does not mean inward repentance only, as there is no inward repentance that does not manifest itself outwardly through various mortifications of the flesh.

4 Luther makes a rather complex point that risks misunderstanding. In his *Explanations* he clarifies his meaning of hating the self: "True sorrow must spring from the goodness and mercies of God, especially from the wounds of Christ, so that man comes first of all to a sense of his own ingratitude in view of divine goodness and thereupon to hatred of himself and love of the kindness of God. Then tears will flow and he will hate himself from the very depths of his heart, yet without despair. Then he will hate sin, not because of the punishment but because of his regard for the goodness of God; and when he has perceived this he will be preserved from despair and will despise himself most ardently, yet joyfully."

5 Luther speaks directly to the pope's authority to pardon sin and remit punishment in purgatory. In the process Luther shows that Tetzel's indulgences are invalid. The word *canons* refers to Canon Law, the body of laws governing the Roman Catholic Church. By Luther's time the canons would encompass various decretals made by the popes and councils. In 1520 Luther publicly burned the *Corpus iurus canonici*, or the Book of Canon Law, along with the papal bull condemning him as a heretic.

6 Medieval Roman Catholic theology distinguished between the concepts of guilt and penalty for sin. Guilt could only be remitted or forgiven by God, whereas the penalty for sin is paid for in either this life or purgatory. Theoretically indulgences were only to satisfy the penalty for sin. Indulgence preachers, however, gave the impression that they also satisfied the guilt for sin.

7 At this time Luther advocates the mediation of a priest. As his theology develops, he moves toward advocating the priesthood of all believers.

8 Luther addresses in theses 8–13 the abusive practices of the sacrament of penance and its corollary, indulgences. The penitential canons, or the church's dogma of penance, restrict penance and forgiveness to eternal punishment. This change in the church's practice is referenced in thesis 11.

4. The penalty of sin, therefore, continues so long as hatred of self, or true inward repentance, continues, and it continues until our entrance into the kingdom of heaven.

5. The pope does not intend to remit, and cannot remit, any penalties except those that he has imposed either by his own authority or by the authority of the canons.

6. The pope cannot remit any guilt, except by declaring that it has been remitted by God and by assenting to God's work of remission. To be sure, however, the pope may grant remission in cases reserved to his judgment. If his right to grant remission in such cases was disregarded, the guilt would remain entirely unforgiven.

7. God remits guilt to no one whom he does not at the same time humble in all things and also bring him into subjection to his vicar, the priest.

8. The penitential canons are imposed only on the living, and according to them nothing should be imposed on the dying.

12 Luther's point draws attention to the fact that forgiveness or absolution theoretically follows contrition and satisfaction. Tetzel's indulgence offers forgiveness without any true sorrow for sin or works of satisfaction.

14 Luther discusses the abuse of penance by focusing on purgatory in theses 14–24. Tetzel's indulgence claimed that it provided "total remission of all sins for souls in purgatory." Luther concludes in thesis 24 that there simply is no basis for this claim.

9. Therefore the Holy Spirit through the pope is kind to us, because in his decrees he always makes exception of the article of death and of necessity.

10. Ignorant and wicked are the acts of those priests who, in the case of the dying, reserve canonical penances for purgatory.

11. This changing of the canonical penalty to the penalty of purgatory is quite evidently one of the tares that were sown while the bishops slept.

12. In former times the canonical penalties were imposed not after but before absolution, as tests of true contrition.

13. The dying are freed by death from all penalties. They are already dead to canonical laws and have a right to be released from them.

14. The imperfect spiritual health, or the imperfect love, of the dying person necessarily brings with it great fear; and the smaller the love, the greater is the fear.

15. This fear and horror is sufficient in itself alone, to say nothing of other things, to constitute the penalty of purgatory, since it is very near to the horror of despair.

16. Hell, purgatory, and heaven seem to differ as do despair, near despair, and the assurance of safety.

17. Concerning souls in purgatory, it seems necessary that horror should grow less and love increase.

21 Though he does not explicitly name Tetzel in the *Ninety-Five Theses*, Luther clearly has him in view when he refers to preachers, or at one point to "hawkers" (thesis 51), of indulgences.

18. It seems unproved, either by reason or Scripture, that they are outside the state of merit, that is, of increasing love.

19. Again, it seems unproved that souls in purgatory, or at least that all of them, are certain or assured of their own blessedness, though we may be quite certain of it.

20. Therefore by "full remission of all penalties" the pope means not actually "of all," but only of those penalties imposed by himself.

21. Therefore those preachers of indulgences are in error, who say that by the pope's indulgences a man is freed from every penalty and is saved.

22. In fact, the pope remits no penalty for the souls in purgatory that, according to the canons, they would have had to pay in this life.

23. If it is at all possible to grant to anyone the remission of all penalties whatsoever, it is certain that this remission can be granted only to the most perfect, that is, to the very few.

24. Therefore, the greater part of the people are necessarily deceived by that indiscriminate and high-sounding promise of release from penalty.

25. The power that the pope has in a general way over purgatory is just like the power that any bishop or curate has in a particular way over his own diocese or parish.

26 The phrase "the power of the keys" refers to the Roman Catholic interpretation of Matthew 16:16–19. By Luther's day this phrase meant the exclusive power given to the church to forgive sin and dispense the blessings and benefits of the gospel. Luther is not denying that the power of the keys primarily resides in the pope. Instead, he is arguing that the pope's exercise of this power does not extend to purgatory.

27 Luther refers to Tetzel's marketing jingle. The phrase was rather catchy in German:

> *Solbald das Geld in Kasten klingt,*
> *Die Seel' aus dem Fegfeuer springt.*
> As soon as the money in the chest rings (klinks),
> A soul from purgatory springs.

29 Luther refers to the legend of two earlier popes, Severinus (638–640) and Paschal I (817–824), which holds that they were willing to endure a longer time of suffering in purgatory in order to enjoy a greater degree of glory in heaven.

32 Luther uses *pardon* interchangeably with *indulgence.*

26. The pope does well when he grants remission to souls in purgatory, not by the power of the keys, which in this case he does not possess, but by way of intercession.

27. They preach man-made doctrines who say that so soon as the coin jingles into the money-box, the soul flies out of purgatory.

28. It is certain that when the coin jingles into the money-box, greed and avarice can be increased, but the result of the intercession of the church is in the power of God alone.

29. Who knows whether all the souls in purgatory wish to be bought out of it, as in the legend of Sts. Severinus and Paschal?

30. No one is sure that his own contrition is sincere, much less that he can attain full remission.

31. As the man who is truly repentant is rare, so rare also is the man who truly buys indulgences. Indeed, such men are most rare.

32. They will be condemned eternally, together with their teachers, who believe themselves sure of their salvation because they have letters of pardon.

33. Men must be on their guard against those who say that the pope's pardons are that inestimable gift of God by which man is reconciled to him;

34. For these graces of pardon concern only the penalties of sacramental satisfaction, and these are appointed by man.

39 This point summarizes the dilemma facing Luther as a parish priest. He had to accept the indulgence letters granted by Tetzel to his own parishioners, yet at the same time he was responsible, as their priest, to remind them of their need of true penance.

42 Luther moves beyond merely presenting arguments for debate in theses 42–51 as he offers his own summary of what Christians should be taught. As a monk he extols the virtues of caring for the poor and needy. He also points out that such virtues conflict with the conspicuous wealth of the papacy.

35. They preach no Christian doctrine who teach that contrition is not necessary in those who intend to buy souls out of purgatory or to buy confessional privileges.

36. Every truly repentant Christian has a right to full remission of penalty and guilt, even without letters of pardon.

37. Every true Christian, whether living or dead, has part in all the benefits of Christ and the church; and this is granted to him by God, even without letters of pardon.

38. Nevertheless, the remission and participation in the benefits of the church, which are granted by the pope, are in no way to be despised, for they are, as I have said, the declaration of divine remission.

39. It is very difficult, even for the most educated theologians, at one and the same time to commend to the people the abundance of pardons and also the need of true contrition.

40. True contrition seeks and loves penalties, but liberal pardons only relax penalties and cause them to be hated, or at least they give a reason for hating them.

41. Papal indulgences are to be preached with caution, so that the people may not falsely think of them as preferable to other good works of love.

42. Christians are to be taught that the pope does not intend the buying of pardons to be compared in any way to works of mercy.

50 This marks the first of several explicit references to the cost of
    building St. Peter's Basilica. Although it is not entirely clear
    to what extent Luther was aware of the dealings of Leo X and
    Albert of Mainz that led to Tetzel's indulgence sale, he and
    others were well aware of the ulterior motive underlying it.

43. Christians are to be taught that he who gives to the poor or lends to the needy does a better work than buying pardons;

44. Because love grows by works of love, man becomes better by doing works of love. By buying pardons, however, man does not grow better, only more free from penalty.

45. Christians are to be taught that he who sees a man in need and passes him by and gives his money for pardons instead, purchases not the indulgences of the pope, but the indignation of God.

46. Christians are to be taught that unless they have more money than they need, they are bound to reserve what is necessary for their own families, and by no means to squander it on pardons.

47. Christians are to be taught that the buying of pardons is a matter of free will, not of commandment.

48. Christians are to be taught that the pope, in granting pardons, needs and therefore desires their devout prayer for him more than their money.

49. Christians are to be taught that the pope's pardons are useful so long as they do not put their trust in them; but altogether harmful if they lose their fear of God because of them.

50. Christians are to be taught that if the pope knew the exactions of the indulgence preachers, he would rather that St. Peter's church should go to ashes than that it should be built up with the skin, flesh, and bones of his sheep.

53 Though far from advocating the Reformation principle of *sola Scriptura* (Scripture alone), Luther emphasizes the necessity and centrality of the Word.

55 The mention of the bell, processions, and ceremonies, as well as the reference to the cross emblazoned with the papal arms in thesis 79, refers to Tetzel's entrance into a city. His arrival was first preceded by the announcement of his coming. He was then escorted to the center of town in a parade flanked by the town's political and ecclesiastical dignitaries. The ceremony was so elaborate that one eyewitness in the town of St. Anneberg records that "God himself could not have been welcomed with greater honor."

56 The phrase "treasures of the church" refers to the medieval Roman Catholic teaching that the surplus merits of Christ and the saints are kept in a heavenly treasury. This explains why Roman Catholics pray to and appeal to saints, especially Mary. In Luther's day the pope could withdraw from this treasury and apply these excess and unused merits to those who fell short and needed more. The withdrawal of merits usually came by way of financial contributions to the church. Luther rejects this whole view outright when he argues in thesis 62 that the true treasure of the church is the gospel.

51. Christians are to be taught that it would be the pope's wish, as it is his duty, to give of his own money to many of those from whom certain hawkers of pardons cajole money, even though the church of St. Peter might have to be sold.

52. The assurance of salvation by letters of pardon is vain, even though the indulgence commissary or the pope himself were to stake his soul upon it.

53. They are enemies of Christ and the pope who bid the Word of God to be silent in some churches in order that pardons may be preached in others.

54. Injury is done to the Word of God when, in the same sermon, an equal or a longer time is spent on pardons than on the Word.

55. It must be the pope's intention that if pardons, which are a very small thing, are celebrated with one bell, single processions, and ceremonies, then the gospel, which is the very greatest thing, should be preached with a hundred bells, a hundred processions, and a hundred ceremonies.

56. The treasures of the church, out of which the pope grants indulgences, are not sufficiently named or known among the people of Christ.

57. That they are not temporal treasures is certainly evident, for many vendors do not pour out such treasures so easily, but only gather them.

58. Nor are they the merits of Christ and the saints, for even without the pope, these always work grace for the inner man, and the cross, death, and hell for the outward man.

59 St. Laurence was martyred in 258. According to legend (now widely rejected), when ordered by Roman officials to turn over the church's riches, he gathered the church's poor.

63 Matthew 20:16 ("So the last shall be first, and the first last"—ASV).

59. St. Laurence said that the treasures of the church were the church's poor, but he spoke according to the usage of the word in his own time.

60. Without being rash we say that the keys of the church, given by Christ's merit, are that treasure;

61. For it is clear that the power of the pope is in itself sufficient for the remission of penalties and of cases reserved for his jurisdiction.

62. The true treasure of the church is the most holy gospel of the glory and grace of God.

63. But this treasure is naturally most odious, for it makes the first to be last.

64. On the other hand, the treasure of indulgences is naturally most acceptable, for it makes the last to be first.

65. Therefore the treasures of the gospel are nets with which they would formerly fish for men of riches.

66. The treasures of the indulgences are nets with which they now fish for the riches of men.

67. The indulgences that the preachers cry as the "greatest graces" are known to be truly such, insofar as they promote gain.

68. In truth, however, they are the absolute smallest graces compared with the grace of God and the piety of the cross.

69. Bishops and curates are bound to admit the commissaries of papal pardons with all reverence.

71 In theses 71–74 Luther affirms indulgences when practiced legitimately, while condemning Tetzel's illegitimate practice of indulgences.

76 Roman Catholic theology distinguishes between venial sins, which can be forgiven, and mortal or deadly sins, which cannot be forgiven.

70. But still more are they bound to strain all their eyes and attend with all their ears, lest these men preach their own dreams instead of the pope's commission.

71. Let him who speaks against the truth of papal pardons be anathema and accursed!

72. But let him who guards against the lust and license of the pardon-preachers be blessed!

73. The pope justly thunders against those who, by any means, contrive harm to the traffic of pardons.

74. But much more does he intend to thunder against those who use the pretext of pardons to contrive injury to holy love and truth.

75. To consider the papal pardons so great that they could absolve a man even if he had committed an impossible sin and violated the Mother of God is madness.

76. We say, on the contrary, that the papal pardons are not able to remove the very least of venial sins, so far as its guilt is concerned.

77. It is said that even St. Peter, if he were now pope, could not bestow greater graces. This is blasphemy against St. Peter and against the pope.

78. We say, on the contrary, that even the present pope, and any pope at all, has greater graces at his disposal: namely, the gospel, powers, gifts of healing, etc., as it is written in 1 Corinthians 12.

81 Luther here introduces a series of "shrewd questions" posed by the laity, which he rehearses in theses 82–89. Evidently the common person was well aware of the scandal of Tetzel's indulgences. Further, these points again reveal the financial motives underlying the indulgence sale as Luther makes explicit reference to the cost of building St. Peter's—a cost, according to thesis 86, born in part by the poor peasants of Germany.

79. To say that the cross emblazoned with the papal arms, which is set up by the preachers of indulgences, is of equal worth with the cross of Christ, is blasphemy.

80. Bishops, curates, and theologians who allow such talk to be spread among the people will have to account for this.

81. This unbridled preaching of pardons makes it difficult, even for learned men, to rescue the reverence due to the pope from slander, or even from the shrewd questions of the laity.

82. Such questions as the following: "Why does the pope not empty purgatory, for the sake of holy love and for the sake of desperate souls that are there, if he redeems an infinite number of souls for the sake of miserable money with which to build a church? The former reasons would be most just, while the latter is most trivial."

83. Or: "Why are funeral and anniversary masses for the dead continued, and why does he not return or permit the withdrawal of the endowments founded on their behalf, since it is wrong to pray for the redeemed?"

84. Or: "What is this new piety of God and the pope, that for money they allow a man who is impious and their enemy to buy out of purgatory the pious soul of a friend of God, and do not rather, because of that pious and beloved soul's own need, free it for pure love's sake?"

86 Leo X (as mentioned in the introduction) was a member of the wealthy and prominent Medici family.

90 Luther's call for "reasonable answers" testifies to his desire for a debate.

85. Or: "Why are the penitential canons, long since in actual fact and through disuse abrogated and dead, now satisfied by the granting of indulgences, as though they were still alive and in force?"

86. Or: "Why does not the pope, whose wealth today is greater than the riches of the richest, build this one basilica of St. Peter with his own money, rather than with the money of poor believers?"

87. Or: "What does the pope remit, and what participation in the benefits of the church does he grant, to those who, by perfect contrition, have a right to full remission and participation?"

88. Or: "What greater blessing could come to the church than if the pope were to do a hundred times a day what he now does once, and bestow on every believer these remissions and participation?"

89. Or finally: "Since the pope, by his pardons, seeks the salvation of souls rather than money, why does he suspend the indulgences and pardons granted prior to now, since these have equal efficacy?"

90. To repress these convincing arguments of the laity by force alone, and not to resolve them by giving reasonable answers, is to expose the church and the pope to the ridicule of their enemies, and to leave Christians unsatisfied.

91. If, therefore, pardons were preached according to the spirit and mind of the pope, all these doubts would be readily resolved. Indeed, they would not exist.

92 Jeremiah 6:14 ("They have healed also the hurt of my people slightly, saying, Peace, peace; when there is no peace"—ASV).

93 Luther's rather poetic ending hints at what would become the very center of his theology: the cross. In this early stage Luther contends that indulgences promise glory without suffering, while he understands Scripture to teach that glory comes only after suffering. Luther ends where he began with the first thesis: challenging the Roman Catholic understanding of repentance and forgiveness, and offering a radical alternative. For more on Luther's theology of the cross, see his *Heidelberg Disputation* (1518).

95 Luther's closing statement underscores that he does not wholly understand justification by faith. By his own admission it would be another two years before his personal theological breakthrough and his recovery of this essential doctrine.

92. Away, then, with all those prophets who say to the people of Christ, "Peace, peace," and there is no peace!

93. Blessed be all those prophets who say to the people of Christ, "Cross, cross," and there is no cross!

94. Christians are to be exhorted to be diligent in following Christ, their Head, through penalties, death, and hell;

95. And thus be confident of entering into heaven through many tribulations, rather than through the false assurance of peace.

For Further Reading

Bainton, Roland H. *Here I Stand: A Life of Martin Luther*. 1950. Reprint ed. New York: Meridian, 1995.

Luther, Martin. *Martin Luther: Selections from His Writings*. Edited by John Dillenberger. Garden City, N.Y.: Doubleday, 1961.

————. *Martin Luther's 95 Theses, with the Pertinent Documents from the History of the Reformation*. Edited by Kurt Aland. St. Louis: Concordia, 1967.

————. *Luther's Works*. Vol. 31, *Career of the Reformer*. Edited by Harold J. Grimm. Philadelphia: Fortress, 1957.

Nichols, Stephen J. *Martin Luther: A Guided Tour of His Life and Thought*. Phillipsburg, N.J.: P&R, 2002.

Stephen J. Nichols (MAR and PhD, Westminster Theological Seminary; MA, West Chester University) is a research professor at Lancaster Bible College and Graduate School. A member of the Evangelical Theological Society, he chairs the society's Jonathan Edwards Study Group.